P9-CCY-027

THE POCKET SCAVENGER

mike

KERI SMITH

A Perigee Book

Create a funny character.

A PERIGEE BOOK
Published by the Penguin Group
Penguin Group (USA) Inc.
375 Hudson Street, New York, New York 10014, USA

USA | Canada | UK | Ireland | Australia | New Zealand | India | South Africa | China

Penguin Books Ltd., Registered Offices: 80 Strand, London WC2R 0RL, England
For more information about the Penguin Group, visit penguin.com.

THE POCKET SCAVENGER

Copyright © 2013 by Keri Smith
All rights reserved. No part of this book may be reproduced, scanned, or distributed in any printed or electronic form without permission. Please do not participate in or encourage piracy of copyrighted materials in violation of the author's rights. Purchase only authorized editions.
PERIGEE is a registered trademark of Penguin Group (USA) Inc.
The "P" design is a trademark belonging to Penguin Group (USA) Inc.

ISBN: 978-0-399-16023-3

First edition: May 2013

PRINTED IN THE UNITED STATES OF AMERICA

10 9 8 7 6543210

Art and design by Keri Smith

While the author has made every effort to provide accurate telephone numbers, Internet addresses, and other contact information at the time of publication, neither the publisher nor the author assumes any responsibility for errors, or for changes that occur after publication. Further, the publisher does not have any control over and does not assume any responsibility for author or third-party websites or their content.

Most Perigee books are available at special quantity discounts for bulk purchases for sales promotions, premiums, fund-raising, or educational use. Special books, or book excerpts, can also be created to fit specific needs. For details, write: Special Markets, Penguin Group (USA) Inc., 375 Hudson Street, New York, New York 10014.

ALWAYS LEARNING PEARSON

Make into a building (house).

THIS BOOK BELONGS TO:

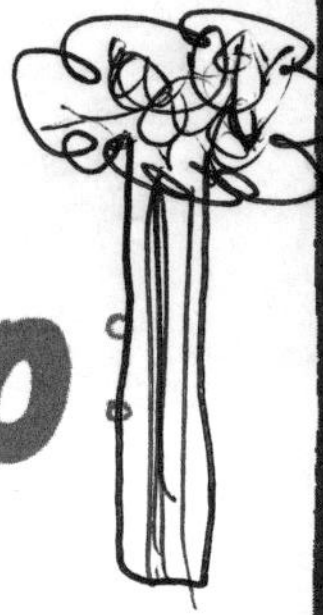

~~Sadie~~ Korinne

WHO IS AN OFFICIAL SCAVENGER AND WORLD EXPLORER.

IF FOUND, PLEASE RETURN TO:

443-946-8365

(ADDRESS, EMAIL OR PHONE #)

SCAVENGING LOCATIONS: house? multiple places!

CODENAME: Sadie

THIS BOOK IS DEDICATED TO ALL THE WORLD'S GREAT TEACHERS. IT ONLY TAKES ONE TO ALTER THE PATH OF A LIFE!

Combine with something from nature.

CONTENTS

INTRODUCTION

COLLECT & ALTER

Turn into a disguise.

Make into a location on a map.

Conceal it.

SOME EXTRA THINGS

Add polka dots.

A SINGLE INANIMATE OBJECT, USELESS IN ITSELF, CAN BE THE FOCUS OF A WORLD.

—YI-FU TUAN

Remove a section.

DEFINITION OF A SCAVENGER

Scavengers…

- go on mini adventures no matter where they are, especially in the most mundane of circumstances
- notice the ground beneath their feet, prowl the world looking for treasures
- see beauty in simple items, when sometimes others do not
- know that all objects can be imbued with special powers
- are interested in transforming simple objects into works of art
- often have collections of items in the bottom of their bag, scattered about their home, or hidden in a yard somewhere
- are always prepared to collect and will go to great lengths to do so, even occasionally putting themselves in precarious situations

COULD THIS BE YOU?

If so, proceed to the next section.

Add stripes.

Scribble on top.

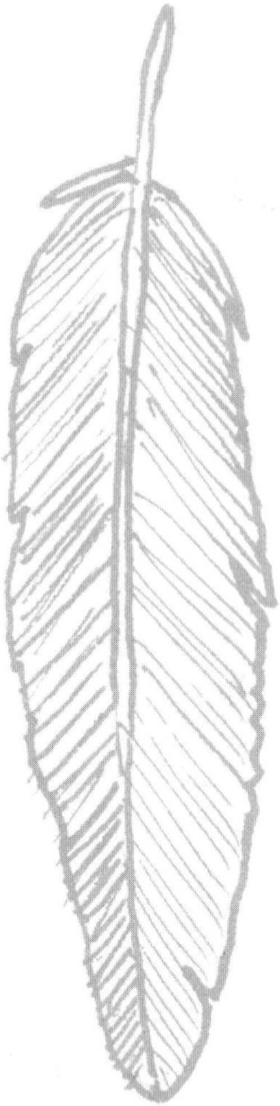

INTRODUCTION

You are invited to go on an adventure—right now, wherever you are.

In the following pages, I'm going to ask you to search for a bunch of items. At first glance, these may seem like simple, mundane, inconsequential things, but don't be fooled—they are of utmost importance!

Every minute of the day there are hundreds (or thousands) of things around us that we don't notice. Our eyes tune them out because they don't seem important for our current needs. But what if we look at every "thing" as if we have never seen it before? As if we do not know its function? In that way, we learn to see it with new eyes.

These things can become very useful if we choose to think of them as raw materials. They are sacred objects just waiting to be collected by a modern-day explorer and used in a variety of artistic experiments.

That is your challenge: to infuse your daily excursions with a quest to see these things with new eyes.

Duplicate it (make a copy).

THE SCAVENGE

The first stage in becoming a natural navigator is to master observation, and the first lesson in this area is that observation is not all about the eyes. And even when it is about the eyes, there is more to it than meets our eyes.
—Tristan Gooley, The Natural Navigator

Most of us have participated in scavenger hunts at some point in our lives: running around a location frantically looking for a set of items typed on a list of some kind, locating the objects before someone else does, finding everything as fast possible.

With the scavenges in this book, we are going to take the act of scavenging into a slightly different realm by first collecting objects and then altering them.

For the first mission, you are going to collect a number of items. They can be found in your immediate environment, on your way to work or school, while you are waiting for the bus, at your local park, while on a hike, while on vacation, and so on. Use the checklist at the back of this book for a quick reference of what to scavenge. For the purposes of this book, you can choose the speed at which you perform the scavenge. You may choose to do it alone. Or you can enlist friends and make it a race.

Fold, cut into pieces, and rearrange.

THE ALTERATION

Once you have an item and are ready for the next step, you will turn the book upside down, flip randomly to a page, read the instruction at the top, and alter the item as instructed. (This is referred to as using "chance" because you do not actively get to choose what alteration you are using. The process of flipping causes you to choose without looking at the alteration first.)

These alterations will allow you to create something entirely new. Think of them as a selection of possibilities for outcomes different than what you would have done if you were given a choice. The alterations are where your genius will come in. Each alteration will be interpreted differently by each person. There is no right or wrong or good or bad in terms of how the alteration is performed. You might love the results; you might find them uninteresting. That is part of the fun—not knowing what will occur.

Turn into an article of clothing.

CHANCE:

1. the occurrence and development of events in the absence of any obvious design : he met his brother by chance | what a lucky chance that you are here. 2. the unplanned and unpredictable course of events regarded as a power : chance was offering me success.

A BRIEF HISTORY OF CHANCE

The use of chance in art began in the 1950s with the artists Ellsworth Kelly, François Morellet, and John Cage. These artists used a variety of methods and techniques including the I Ching, grid systems (assigning random colors to the squares), dot systems, random sampling on a computer, dice, using gravity (falling, dropping, dripping), chance meetings, etc.

Trace it and use the shape as basis for a new drawing.

So often when we are creating something—a piece of art, a piece of writing, a musical composition—we do what has worked for us in the past, what we are the best at, what is current, what is reliable, what is obvious, what we think is good. But this method tends to make our work repetitive and stale. Creativity arises from our ability to see things from many different angles. New connections (things that have not been connected before) create new ideas.

Incorporating chance into the exercise allows us to make connections and try things that we might not have done on our own. We are forced out of our habitual ways of thinking or acting.

Chance is beloved of Art, and Art of Chance.

–Agathon, fragments (c. 415 B.C.), quoted by Aristotle

?

Make it pretty.

THE BENEFITS AND JOYS OF BEING A SCAVENGER

I devote a day to creating a kind of "story." Walking down, say, Sixth Avenue, I'll suddenly see something that intrigues me—a plastic bag, a green umbrella, an airplane tracing a line in the sky. That's how I get started.
—Gabriel Orozco (on recent films, 1998)

1. The process of collecting tunes us into our environment and makes use of our increasingly underused senses. You may begin to see that everything is interesting.

2. In our current culture of immediacy, we have lost the experience of "the quest," the search for that elusive item and the stories we create in our attempt to find it. These stories, the process (vs. the object itself), are often what make life interesting.

3. Scavenging is fun and addictive (and much better for us than watching screens all day), especially when done with others and when you share your unique results.

4. Living in a consumerist society, it is easy to get caught up in a lifestyle that is just about shopping or is connected to a corporate entity. This leaves us feeling empty and causes a discon-

Combine with page 14.

nect with the natural world. It is important for us to participate in activities that open us up to exploring the world around us on a regular basis without a focus on money/commerce. Tuning into our immediate environment also serves to make us feel more connected to the natural world.

5. You will never be at a loss for materials for artistic endeavors.

What if we begin to see the world as alive and animate? What if every item told a story?

With The Pocket Scavenger, what emerges will be entirely different for every person who works with the book. Each version will be based on a variety of factors, our life experiences, our location, our culture, chance, and how we interpret the ideas. Working with items in this way will help train our brains to look at things without preconceived ideas. Over time we will naturally make new connections and formulate new patterns of thinking. We will develop a habit of "trying something new" or different.

AN IMPORTANT NOTE:

SOMETIMES THE RESULT WILL BE INTERESTING AND SOMETIMES IT WON'T. THAT IS THE NATURE OF AN EXPERIMENT.

Clean it up.

SCAVENGER TOOLS

YOU WILL NEED:

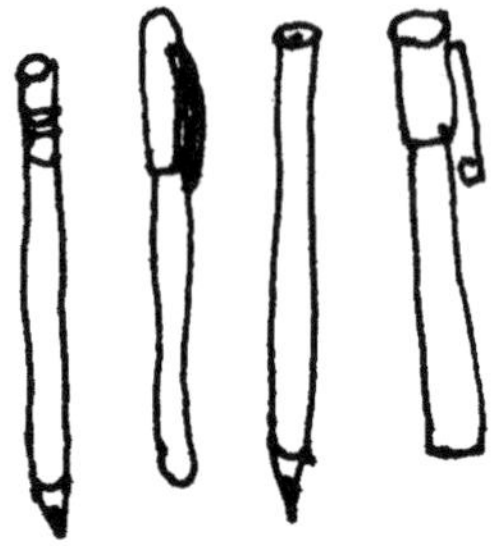

ERASER CHALK SCISSORS

PAINT

A VARIETY OF WRITING AND DRAWING UTENSILS

A SELECTION OF ART MATERIALS

COFFEE
TEA

SAND PAPER

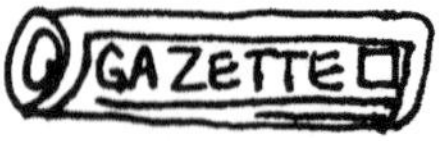

GAZETTE

NEWSPAPER MUD

SOME NON-ART MATERIALS*

* SEE LIST OF ALTERATION MATERIALS ON THE NEXT PAGE.

VARIOUS WAYS TO STORE THINGS UNTIL YOU CAN AFFIX THEM INTO THE BOOK. ATTACH AN ENVELOPE TO THE INSIDE OF THE BACK COVER TO STORE THINGS TEMPORARILY WHEN YOU ARE OUT ON SCAVENGES.

A "SCAVENGING UNIFORM" OF SOME KIND, SOMETHING THAT HELPS GET YOU INTO THE MIND-SET.

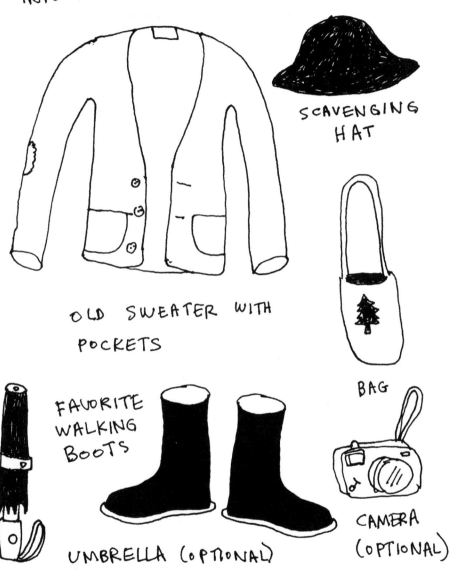

SCAVENGING HAT

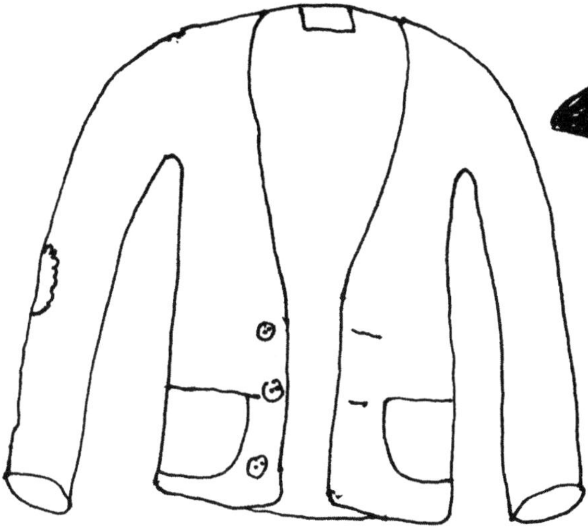

OLD SWEATER WITH POCKETS

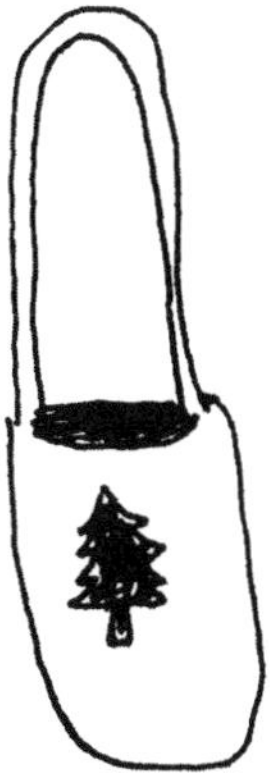

BAG

CAMERA (OPTIONAL)

FAVORITE WALKING BOOTS

UMBRELLA (OPTIONAL)

Turn it upside down. What does it look like now?

ATTACHMENT METHODS:

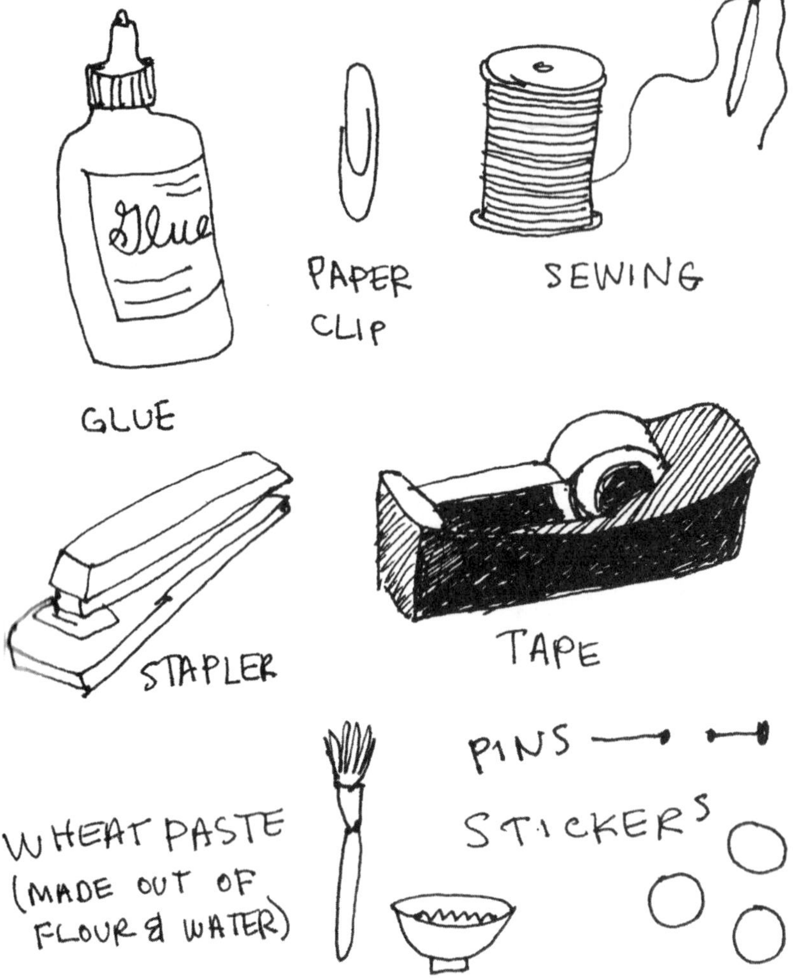
Glue
GLUE
PAPER CLIP
SEWING
STAPLER
TAPE
WHEAT PASTE (MADE OUT OF FLOUR & WATER)
PINS
STICKERS

NOTE: SOME ITEMS MAY SEEM A LITTLE BULKY FOR THE BOOK. THIS IS TO BE EXPECTED. YOU MAY HAVE TO PUT A LARGE ELASTIC BAND AROUND IT TO KEEP IT CONTAINED.

Make it scary.

ALTERATION MATERIALS YOU MAY LIKE TO USE...

HAMMER
SCISSORS
PAINT BRUSH
PEN
PENCIL
PIN
INK
WATER
WATER BASED PAINT
ACRYLI
CHARCOAL
STICKS
WHITE GLUE
TAPE
PAPER
COFFEE/TEA
CRAYON
CRAYON
CRAYONS
FOUND PHOTO
PAPER BAG
FOOD
KETCHUP
SANDPAPER
STONES
CHALK
GAZETTE
MAGAZINE OR NEWSPAPER
ELASTIC BAND
STRAW
PUSH PINS
LEAVES
DIRT
PLASTIC BAGS
CEREAL
CARDBOARD
FABRIC
STRING
ERASER
ASH
1
COIN
MARKERS
*ANYTHING ELSE YOU CAN THINK OF.

SCAVENGING TIPS

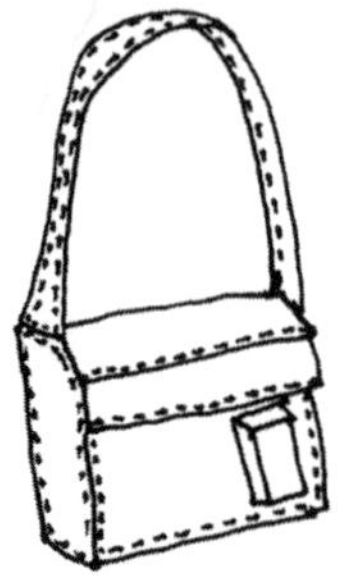

- Get in the habit of looking around while wandering in your neighborhood. Scan the ground for finds. Some things you will find quickly, or know exactly where to look. Others will take some time and require ingenuity and serendipity. Occasionally you will come upon something when you least expect it (e.g., while walking to work, you spot a piece of red string on the sidewalk); these are the most interesting finds and make the best stories. Write about it on the object's page.

- Recruit your friends and family to help you (if you choose).

- Enjoy the process. Scavenging works best when you are fully immersed in the moment.

- Memorize (or familiarize) yourself with the list of items to scavenge, so you will be working on it as you go about your day.

- Try navigating your environment in a non-linear fashion, or take different routes than you normally do. You may discover new things this way.

IMPORTANT NOTE: You will want to avoid any items that are sharp, dangerous-looking, or toxic. (Avoid standing water or unknown substances.) If you are unsure if an item is okay, it is best to leave it behind.

Add some kind of explosion.

ALTERATION TIPS

- Be willing to try something just to see what happens—even if you don't think you will like it. You may come up with the most interesting stuff this way! Get into the habit of experimenting.

- If you come upon a wild card you may pick an alteration of your choosing, or you can just flip again.

- Try working with as many different materials as you can. So for example, if the alteration says "add dots" you could use paint, coffee, gum, collage, or anything else you can think of!

- If you are prone to cheating, dare yourself to do as instructed.

- If you really dislike what you created, you have permission to repeat the whole process or transform it into something else entirely.

Bonus tip: You may like to use the alterations in this book for other projects you are working on.

Add warmth.

INSTRUCTIONS

1. Take this book with you everywhere you go.

2. Find/collect the things on each page. Affix them somehow to the left-hand side of the page.* Fill in the notes about where you found the item. Under "story" you can describe the circumstances surrounding the scavenge.** You may also choose to write an imaginary story about the item.

3. For each collected item, turn the book upside down and randomly flip to a page. Alter it as directed. How you interpret each alteration is up to you.

4. Share your alterations with others using your preferred method (social network, art show, trade book with friends, etc.).

*You may also choose to take photos of the items, but you must find a way to print them so you can alter them later.

**Remember that these items may not seem that important on their own, but in your collecting of them, they will become valuable treasures. You will become the envy of all your friends!

Group several items together.

THE WAY EACH PERSON CHOOSES ITEMS AND WORKS WITH THEM WILL BE UNIQUE.

Add some text.

SCAVENGER MAP

Draw a detailed map of your neighborhood. Document on the map all of the locations at which you found your scavenged items. Create your own legend.

Simplify it.

LEGEND

It's a hat.

1

POSTAGE STAMPS

CALL ME
TRIMTAB

LOCATION FOUND: ______________

TIME: ________ DATE: ________

STORY: ______________________

____

____

____

____

____

____

____

____

____

____

Flip three pages ahead—follow those directions.

2

Do nothing.

2

THE NUMBER FIVE

5

LOCATION FOUND: Airport

TIME: 6:44 am DATE: 4/19/12

STORY: I was looking aroud the airport and I found 1-5 line!

Alter the edges.

Make item the background for something else.

3

PAPER CLIP

LOCATION FOUND: ____________

TIME: ______ DATE: ________

STORY: ______________________

____

____

____

____

____

____

____

____

____

____

Wild card. Choose an alteration yourself.

Add some texture.

4

A FEATHER

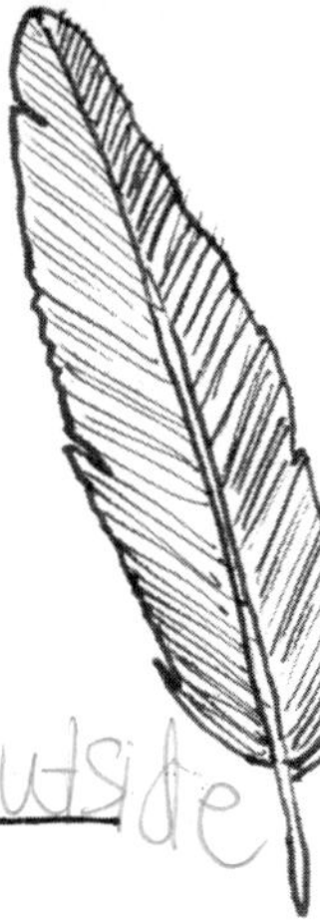

LOCATION FOUND: the deck outside

TIME: 6:24 DATE: 9/6/19

STORY: I was outside looking for stuff to write in here!

Make holes.

Ask a friend what you should do.

5

A USED ENVELOPE

K. SMITH
P.O. BOX 92
SOMEWHERE
USA
CURRENT RESIDENT
11 RUE SIMON-CRUBELLIER
PARIS, FRANCE
75017

LOCATION FOUND: bedroom

TIME: 6:27 DATE: 9/5/19

STORY: I was looking through my birthday cards and found this!

Add legs.

Cut into strips.

6

A TICKET

INSTRUCTIONS
CLAIM # 978-1-59017-313-

LOCATION FOUND: Airport

TIME: 6:47am DATE: 4/~~2~~19/19

STORY: I was looking threw the airport for a ticket and I got a airplane ticket!

Combine with a photo.

Add ten colors.

7

NINE CIRCLES

LOCATION FOUND: Kitchen/livingroom

TIME: 6:28 DATE: 9/15/19

STORY: I found 7 circles aka lights and sprinklers!

Invent an animal.

Make a self-portrait.

8

TEN DOLLARS DIX
10
OTTAWA

A FORM OF CURRENCY

LOCATION FOUND: ____________

TIME: ______ DATE: ________

STORY: ____________

Alter the space around the item (not the item itself).

Add a series of diverging lines.

9

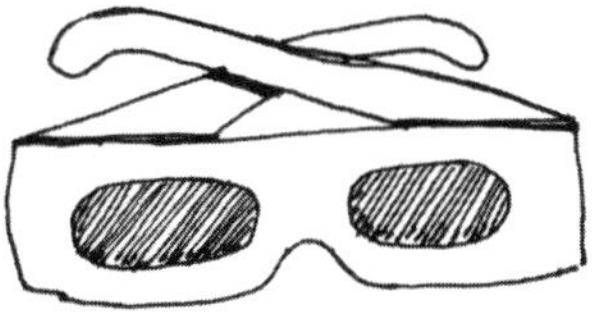

SOMETHING YOU CAN SEE THROUGH

LOCATION FOUND: bedroom

TIME: 12:52pm DATE: April, 7th, 2020

STORY: I got the glasses at CVS to have fake glasses.

Add a color you dislike.

Fill the entire space.

10

THREE DIFFERENT TEXTURES

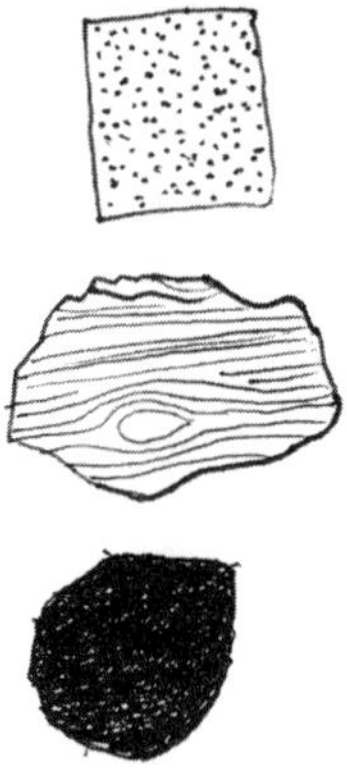

LOCATION FOUND: bedroom

TIME: 12:54 DATE: April, 7th, 2020

STORY: I found something soft, smooth, and bumpy.

Frame it.

Add transparent/translucent layers.

11

SOMETHING WITH TEXT ON IT

The magician's underwear has just been found in a cardboard suitcase floating in a stagnant pond on the outskirts of

LOCATION FOUND: ____________

TIME: ________ DATE: ________

STORY: ____________

Delete the middle.

Do something your hero would do.

12

A POST-IT NOTE

READ THIS.

LOCATION FOUND: ____________

TIME: ______ DATE: ________

STORY: ______________________

Smudge something over it with your fingers.

Crumple it.

13

A PIECE OF MOSS

LOCATION FOUND: ____________

TIME: ______ DATE: ________

STORY: ____________

Soak with water.

Add scratches.

14

SOME WIRE

LOCATION FOUND: ____________

TIME: ______ DATE: __________

STORY: ____________________

____

____

____

____

____

____

____

____

____

____

Add a series of triangles.

Turn into a landscape.

15

A PART OF SOMETHING YOU ATE

LOCATION FOUND: ______________

TIME: ______ DATE: ______

STORY: ______________

Draw a box.

Place in a location where it will get dirty.

16

SOMETHING YOU CAN ONLY FIND IN YOUR LOCAL ENVIRONMENT

LOCATION FOUND: ____________

TIME: ______ DATE: ______

STORY: ____________

____

____

____

____

____

____

____

____

____

____

Lose the item.

Drip coffee or tea on it.

17

SOMETHING ON YOUR BODY

RECEIPT
0-679-
42299-4

LOCATION FOUND: ______________

TIME: ________ DATE: __________

STORY: ______________________

____

____

____

____

____

____

____

____

____

____

Drip paint on it.

Make it funny.

18

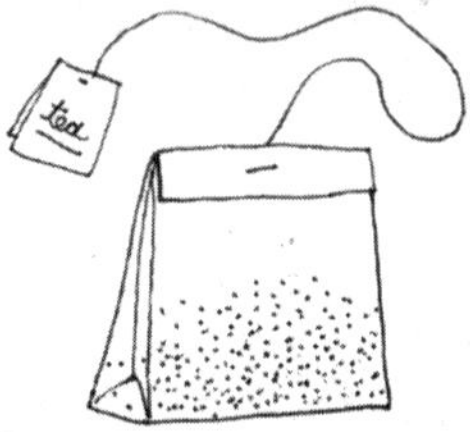
tea

A USED TEA BAG

LOCATION FOUND: ____________

TIME: ______ DATE: ________

STORY: ____________________

____

____

____

____

____

____

____

____

____

____

Scribble with your eyes closed.

Chop it up.

19

A NAPKIN

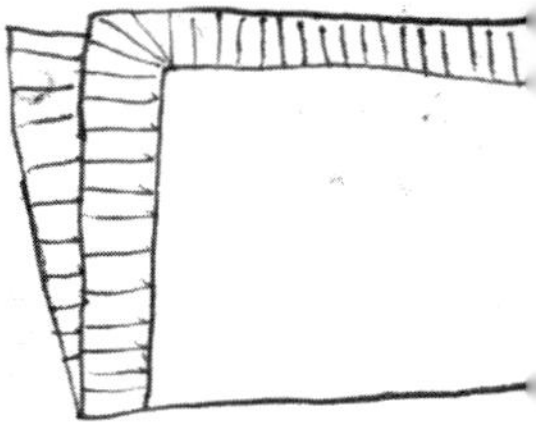

LOCATION FOUND: __________
TIME: ______ DATE: ________
STORY: ________________

Make it political.

Make it obscured.

20

SOMETHING STICKY

HELLO
MY NAME IS:

LOCATION FOUND: ____________

TIME: ______ DATE: ________

STORY: ______________________

Add string.

Turn it into something else.

21

SIX BLUE THINGS

LOCATION FOUND: ____________

TIME: ______ DATE: ________

STORY: ____________________

Change the perspective.

Turn it into something you love.

22

A PIECE OF A PUZZLE

LOCATION FOUND: ____________

TIME: ______ DATE: ________

STORY: ____________

Drag it along a rough surface.

44

Smear something onto it.

23

AN ELASTIC BAND

LOCATION FOUND: ____________

TIME: ______ DATE: ________

STORY: ____________________

____

____

____

____

____

____

____

____

____

____

Cut out some bits of paper. Glue them on.

Add some thumbprints.

24

AN IMAGE OF A CHARACTER

LOCATION FOUND: ______________

TIME: ________ DATE: __________

STORY: ______________________

Add circles.

Draw the opposite.

25

SEVERAL KINDS OF LEAVES

LOCATION FOUND: ______________

TIME: ______ DATE: __________

STORY: ______________________

Consider it complete.

Turn it into a story.

26

A PIECE OF RED STRING

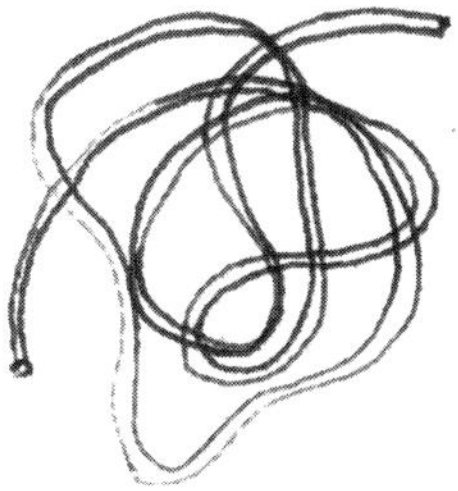

LOCATION FOUND: ______________

TIME: ________ DATE: __________

STORY: ______________________

____

____

____

____

____

____

____

____

____

____

What sound would it make?

Turn it into a vehicle.

27

A WRAPPER

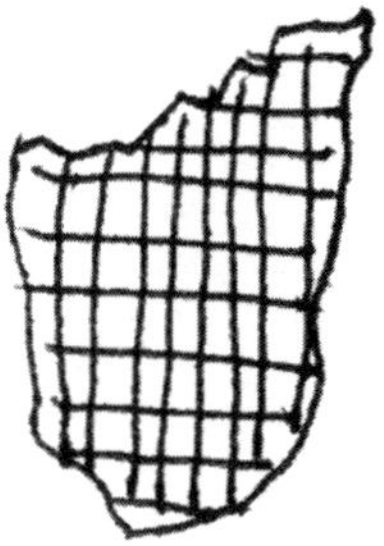

LOCATION FOUND: ____________

TIME: ______ DATE: ________

STORY: ____________________

____

____

____

____

____

____

____

____

____

____

Frame it.

Age it.

28

A PHOTO OF YOURSELF

LOCATION FOUND: ____________

TIME: ______ DATE: ________

STORY: ________________________

____

____

____

____

____

____

____

____

____

____

Wild card. Choose an alteration yourself.

Add eyes.

29

THERE ARE SO MANY JOYS,
AND I HAVE ONLY KNOWN
THE ONES THAT COME
LIKE A MIRACLE AND
TOUCH ORDINARY LIFE
WITH LIGHT. ANAÏS NIN

A POSTCARD

LOCATION FOUND: ____________

TIME: ________ DATE: ________

STORY: ____________

Add tape.

Color outside the lines.

30

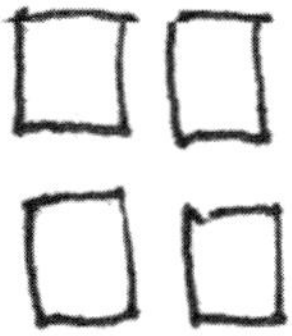

FOUR SQUARES

LOCATION FOUND: ______________

TIME: ________ DATE: __________

STORY: ______________________

Add some music.

Make it REALLY funny.

31

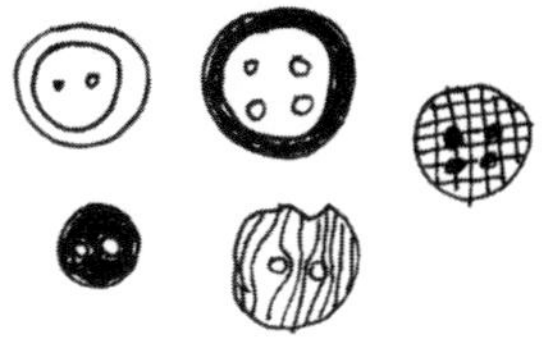

FIVE BUTTONS

LOCATION FOUND: ____________

TIME: ______ DATE: ________

STORY: ________________

Turn it into a math equation.

Turn it into a pattern (repeat it).

32

AN IMAGE OF AN ELEPHANT

LOCATION FOUND: ____________

TIME: ______ DATE: ________

STORY: ____________________

Attach something else.

Add a newspaper clipping.

33

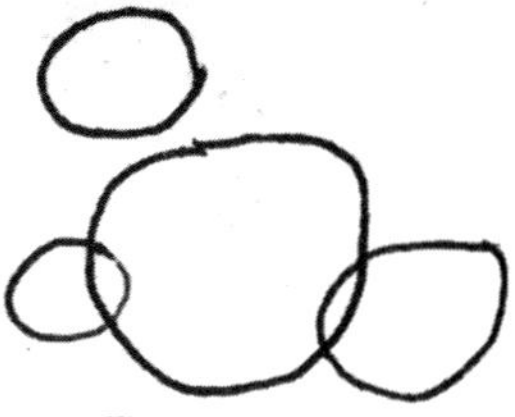

ROCK TRACINGS

LOCATION FOUND: ____________

TIME: ______ DATE: ________

STORY: ____________________

____

____

____

____

____

____

____

____

____

____

Spatter it.

Stencil something over top (a word or a shape).

34

SOMETHING ORANGE

LOCATION FOUND: ____________

TIME: ________ DATE: __________

STORY: ______________________

____

____

____

____

____

____

____

____

____

____

Add fog.

Add exactly six lines/marks.

35

5 CENTS
CANADA
1970

SOMETHING FROM THE YEAR YOU WERE BORN

LOCATION FOUND: ____________

TIME: ______ DATE: ________

STORY: ________________

Add a grid.

Cover with chalk. Remove some.

YOU HAVE A FLANNEL UNDERSHIRT.

36

A HANDWRITTEN QUOTE

LOCATION FOUND: ______________

TIME: ________ DATE: __________

STORY: ______________________

____

____

____

____

____

____

____

____

____

____

Play.

Scratch.

37

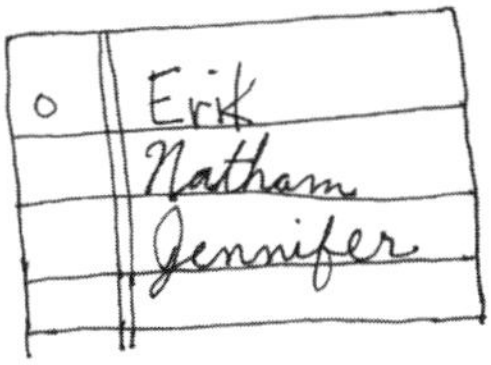
Erik
Jennifer

SAMPLES OF HANDWRITING FROM FIVE DIFFERENT PEOPLE

LOCATION FOUND: ____________

TIME: ______ DATE: ________

STORY: ____________

Add one never-ending line.

38

A PENCIL RUBBING OF A GRAVESTONE

JORGE LUIS BORGES
...AND NE FORBEDON NA

LOCATION FOUND: ______________

TIME: ______ DATE: ________

STORY: ______________________

What memory does it spark? Write about it.

Turn into an adventure.

39

A HAIR SAMPLE

LOCATION FOUND: ______________

TIME: ________ DATE: __________

STORY: ______________________

____

____

____

____

____

____

____

____

____

____

Add a shadow.

Write five questions about the item.

40

YOU WILL SOON MAKE A FRIEND.

A FORTUNE FROM A FORTUNE COOKIE

LOCATION FOUND: ______________

TIME: ________ DATE: ____________

STORY: ________________________

____

____

____

____

____

____

____

____

____

____

Add some very tiny, almost imperceptible decoration.

08

Turn into a badge.

41

COUPON
#0-14-130 115-5
GREETINGS TO YOU, THE
LUCKY FINDER OF THIS COUPON.

A COUPON

LOCATION FOUND: ____________

TIME: ______ DATE: ________

STORY: ____________________

____

____

____

____

____

____

____

____

____

____

Turn into a magical object.

Wild card. Choose an alteration yourself.

42

SOMETHING THAT IS BROKEN OR DAMAGED

LOCATION FOUND: ____________

TIME: ______ DATE: ________

STORY: ____________________

____

____

____

____

____

____

____

____

____

____

Invent a story.

Add a color based on a memory association with the item.

43

SOMETHING THAT WAS DISCARDED

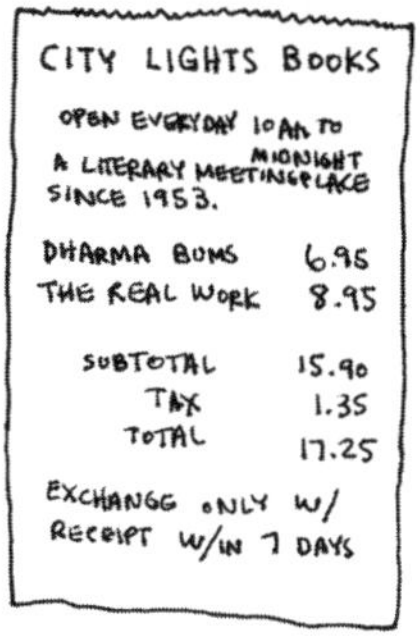
CITY LIGHTS BOOKS
OPEN EVERYDAY 10AM TO MIDNIGHT
A LITERARY MEETINGPLACE SINCE 1953.
DHARMA BUMS 6.95
THE REAL WORK 8.95
SUBTOTAL 15.90
TAX 1.35
TOTAL 17.25
EXCHANGG ONLY W/ RECEIPT W/IN 7 DAYS

LOCATION FOUND: ____________

TIME: ______ DATE: __________

STORY: ______________________

____

____

____

____

____

____

____

____

____

____

Write an ode to this item.

44

A STAIN MADE BY A LIQUID

LOCATION FOUND: ____________

TIME: ______ DATE: ________

STORY: ____________

Combine with another found item.

Add your favorite color in abundance.

45

A STAIN THAT IS GREEN

LOCATION FOUND: ____________

TIME: ______ DATE: ________

STORY: ____________________

____

____

____

____

____

____

____

____

____

____

06

Add a pattern.

46

SOMETHING THAT CAN BE CRUMBLED

LOCATION FOUND: ____________

TIME: ______ DATE: ________

STORY: ____________________

____

____

____

____

____

____

____

____

____

____

Turn into a floorplan.

Combine with a leaf.

47

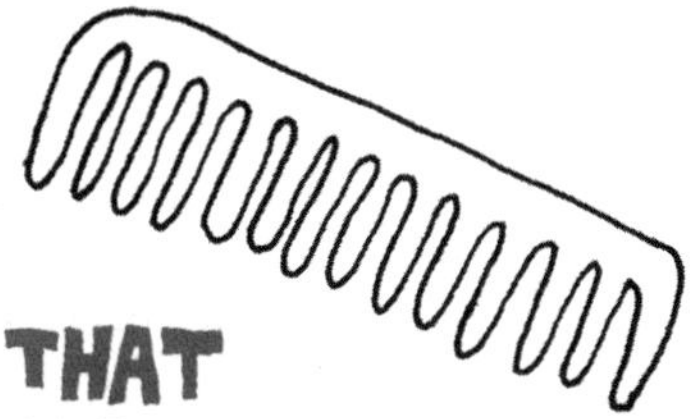

SOMETHING THAT CAN BE DRAGGED AND LEAVES A MARK

LOCATION FOUND: ____________

TIME: ______ DATE: ________

STORY: ____________

____

____

____

____

____

____

____

____

____

____

Add some cracks.

Add stitches.

48

SOMETHING THAT WAS PART OF A TREE

LOCATION FOUND: ____________

TIME: ______ DATE: ________

STORY: ____________

____

____

____

____

____

____

____

____

____

____

Add some triangles.

Make it inviting.

49

SOMETHING THAT WAS PLANTED

LOCATION FOUND: ____________

TIME: ______ DATE: ________

STORY: ____________

____

____

____

____

____

____

____

____

____

____

Make it dark.

Connect this item to an item you love.

50

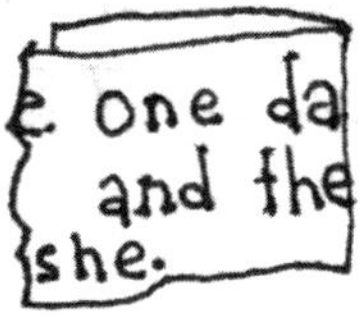
e. one da
and the
she.

A FOUND NOTE

LOCATION FOUND: __________

TIME: _____ DATE: ________

STORY: ____________________

Dream up a scenario.

Take in a different direction.

51

A PIECE OF FLAT CANDY

LOCATION FOUND: __________

TIME: ______ DATE: ______

STORY: __________

What would you have done at age five?

Add another dimension.

52

A FEW SEED PODS

LOCATION FOUND: ______________

TIME: ______ DATE: __________

STORY: ______________________

____

____

____

____

____

____

____

____

____

____

Rearrange.

Drip and blow ink.

53

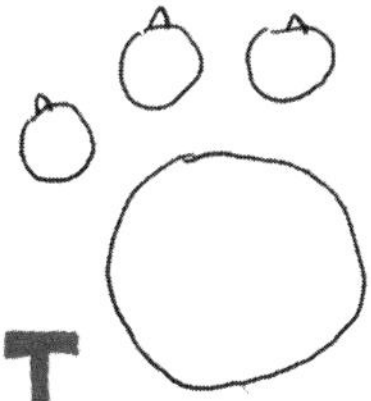

SOMETHING LEFT BY AN ANIMAL

LOCATION FOUND: ______________

TIME: ________ DATE: __________

STORY: ______________________

____

____

____

____

____

____

____

____

____

____

Wrinkle.

Cut in half.

54

Drink Me!

SOMETHING THAT WAS CREATED USING A MACHINE

LOCATION FOUND: ______________

TIME: ________ DATE: ________

STORY: ______________

____

____

____

____

____

____

____

____

____

____

Paint with your finger.

Drop string that has ink on it (make a print).

What story down there awaits its end?

55

SOMETHING THAT WAS MADE BY HAND

LOCATION FOUND: ______________

TIME: ________ DATE: ______________

STORY: ______________________________

Rub surface with dirt.

Squirt ink (or another colored liquid).

56

SOMETHING THAT IS MINIATURE

LOCATION FOUND: ____________

TIME: ______ DATE: ________

STORY: ________________

Paint it red.

Add several blobs of glue.

57

A PIECE OF ORIGAMI

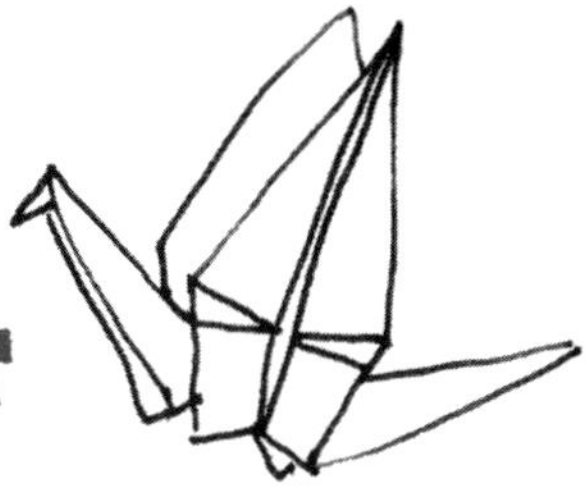

LOCATION FOUND: ____________

TIME: ________ DATE: ____________

STORY: ______________________

____

____

____

____

____

____

____

____

____

____

Wild card. Choose an alteration yourself.

Turn into a monster.

58

SOMETHING THAT WAS GIVEN TO YOU

LOCATION FOUND: ____________

TIME: ______ DATE: ________

STORY: ______________

____

____

____

____

____

____

____

____

____

____

Turn into an odd character.

Add a pencil rubbing texture.

59

A DRAWING (NOT DONE BY YOU)

LOCATION FOUND: ____________

TIME: ______ DATE: ________

STORY: ______________________

Add something that is blown across the surface.

Turn into an island.

60

SEVERAL DIFFERENT KINDS OF GRASS

LOCATION FOUND: ____________

TIME: ______ DATE: ________

STORY: ____________________

____

____

____

____

____

____

____

____

____

____

Alter the shape.

Print something onto it.

61

SOMETHING THAT IS IMAGINARY

LOCATION FOUND: ______________

TIME: ________ DATE: ________

STORY: ______________________

____

____

____

____

____

____

____

____

____

____

Make it into a boat.

Combine several alterations of your choosing.

62

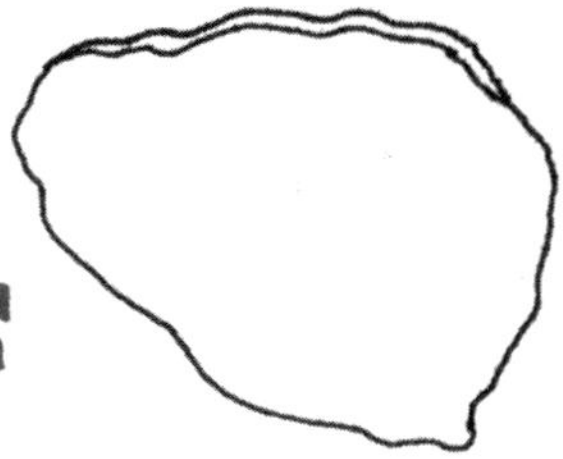

A PIECE OF STYROFOAM

LOCATION FOUND: ____________

TIME: ________ DATE: ________

STORY: ____________________

____

____

____

____

____

____

____

____

____

____

Do something really fast without thinking.

Turn it into a machine/device.

63

SEVERAL PLASTIC ITEMS OF DIFFERENT COLORS

LOCATION FOUND: ____________

TIME: ______ DATE: ________

STORY: ______________

Add some movement.

64

SOMETHING WITH SPOTS

LOCATION FOUND: ______________

TIME: ________ DATE: __________

STORY: ______________________

Let your gut tell you what to do.

Draw in the same direction as the wind.

65

SOMETHING CURVED

LOCATION FOUND: ____________

TIME: ______ DATE: ________

STORY: ____________________

Add colored paper.

Do some crosshatching.

66

SIX TRIANGLES

LOCATION FOUND: ____________

TIME: ______ DATE: ________

STORY: ____________________

____

____

____

____

____

____

____

____

____

____

Add an explosion.

Draw it as you see it.

67 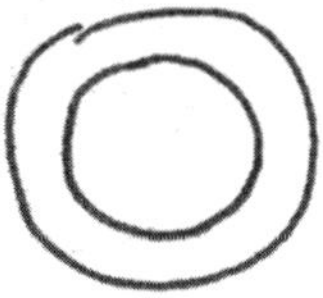

SOMETHING WITH A HOLE IN IT

LOCATION FOUND: ____________

TIME: ________ DATE: ________

STORY: ____________________

____

____

____

____

____

____

____

____

____

____

Turn it into a sign.

68

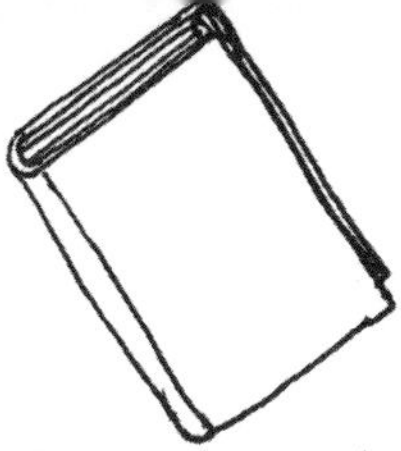

A PART OF A BOOK

LOCATION FOUND: ______________

TIME: ________ DATE: __________

STORY: ____________________

____

____

____

____

____

____

____

____

____

____

Add something orange.

Combine with an everyday object.

69

A PENCIL RUBBING OF THE BOTTOM OF A SHOE

LOCATION FOUND: ____________

TIME: ________ DATE: ____________

STORY: ______________________________

Do something you never do.

Make it white.

70

SOMETHING FROM A CONSTRUCTION SITE

LOCATION FOUND: ____________

TIME: ______ DATE: __________

STORY: ______________________

____

____

____

____

____

____

____

____

____

____

Turn it into something else.

Re-create it in another material.

71

50995
9 780671 69588 0

A UPC SYMBOL

LOCATION FOUND: ____________

TIME: ______ DATE: ________

STORY: ______________

Place it into a new environment.

Add an arrow (or a series of arrows).

72

A PIECE OF GREEN FABRIC

LOCATION FOUND: ______________

TIME: ________ DATE: ____________

STORY: ______________________

Add clouds.

Smudge pencil lines with your finger.

SOME EXTRA THINGS

(FURTHER SCAVENGING)

Trim into new shape.

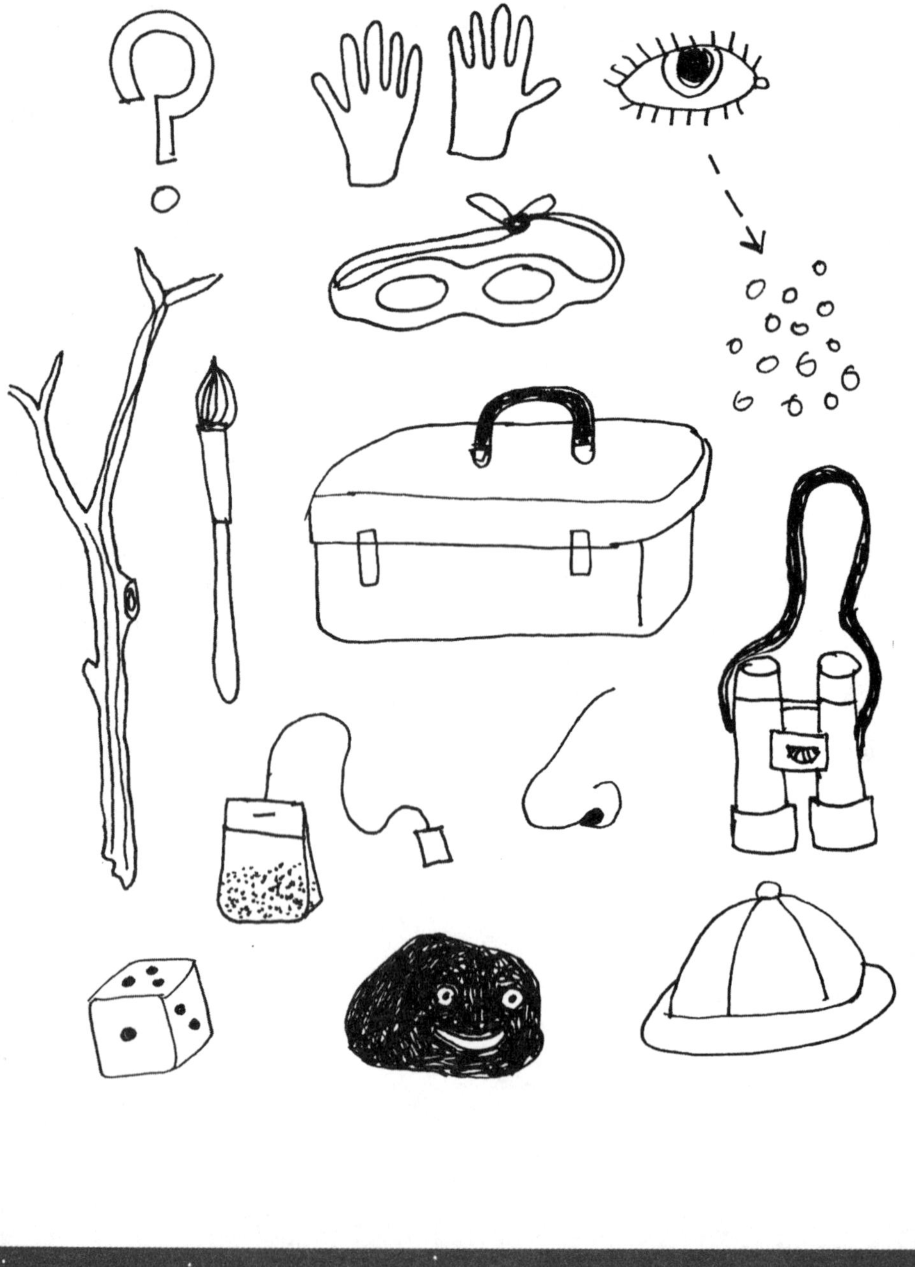

Trace shapes over top.

FUN THINGS TO DO

•Play a game with two or more people. Assign an item for everyone to collect. Then have everyone use the same alteration. Impose a time limit for the alteration. Compare results.

•Try doing several alterations to each item. You may wish to roll a die to tell you how many alterations to employ.

•Try completing all of the collecting at once, and then begin the alterations.

•Try collecting multiples of one of the items and experimenting with many different alterations (or combinations of alterations).

•Make an exhibit with your items. Create a mini museum in a public forum.

•Start a scavenger flash mob. Invite people to do a public scavenger hunt on a social network.

•Create your own scavenges. Hide things for a friend to find on their way to school/work.

•Conduct a scavenging workshop, or create a club. Pick a new item to find every week.

•Take the things you have collected and explore them further. Conduct research. Trace the origins. Look at them from many different perspectives, shape, color, texture, history, etc. Pretend you are new to the planet. What do these items tell you about the inhabitants of earth?

•Take your altered items and create some kind of narrative based on them.

•Experiment with the scavenges on the following pages.

Give it an interesting title or caption.

MATCHES

Turn it into a mask.

RANDOM SCAVENGE

1. Take a walk in your neighborhood.

2. Collect twenty things you find on your walk.

3. Document them on a map. Write a story about each item.

Add a black shape.

CARDBOARD
KEY RING
TAG
STONE WITH LINE ON IT
BLUE RIBBON
UPC CODE
GRASS
ACORN CAP
BUTTON
GREEN LEAF

Combine with another object.

Tear shapes out of paper to add.

ROBIN
GRRR
CONVER-
SATION
LAUGHTER

Add a dotted line.

Add a yellow object.

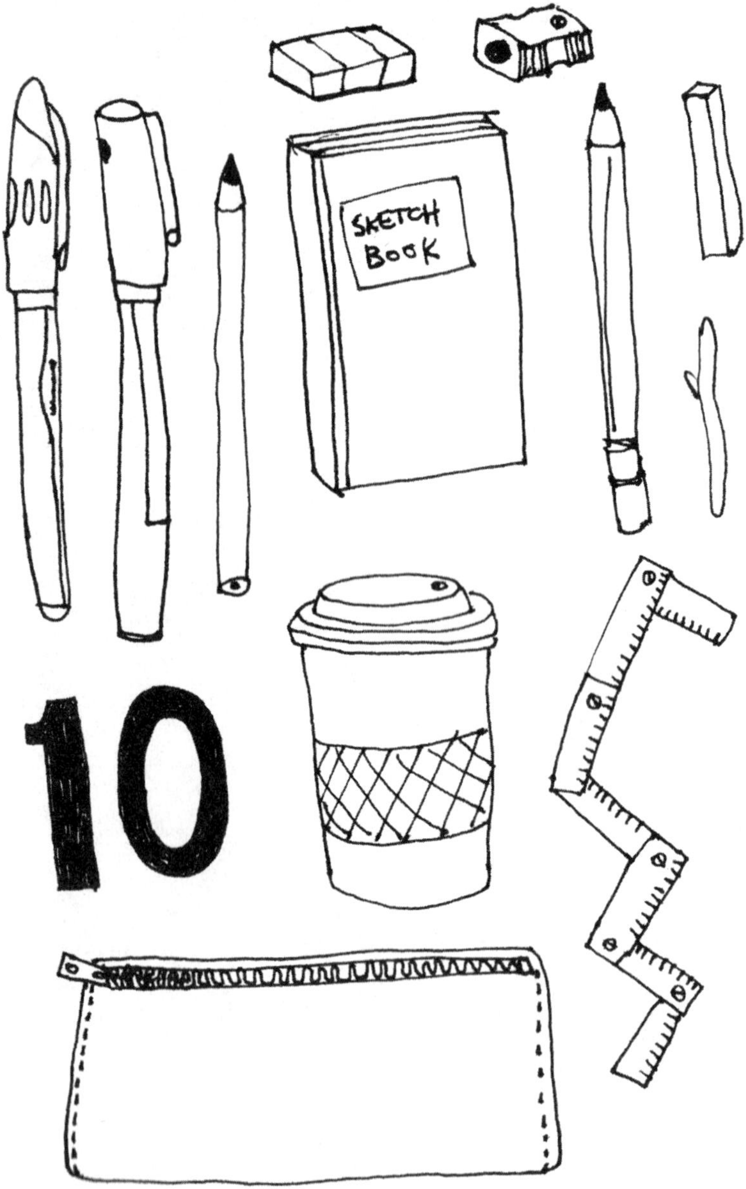
SKETCH
BOOK

Add something shiny.

SKETCH SCAVENGE

1. Go for a walk in a predetermined location.

2. Sketch ten items you find.

3. Document the locations on a map.

Add a crooked line.

AbcDe
fGhijk
LmNop
QRstu
VWXyZ

Add a blob.

Find and add something with a similar shape.

Draw the outline of a tree.

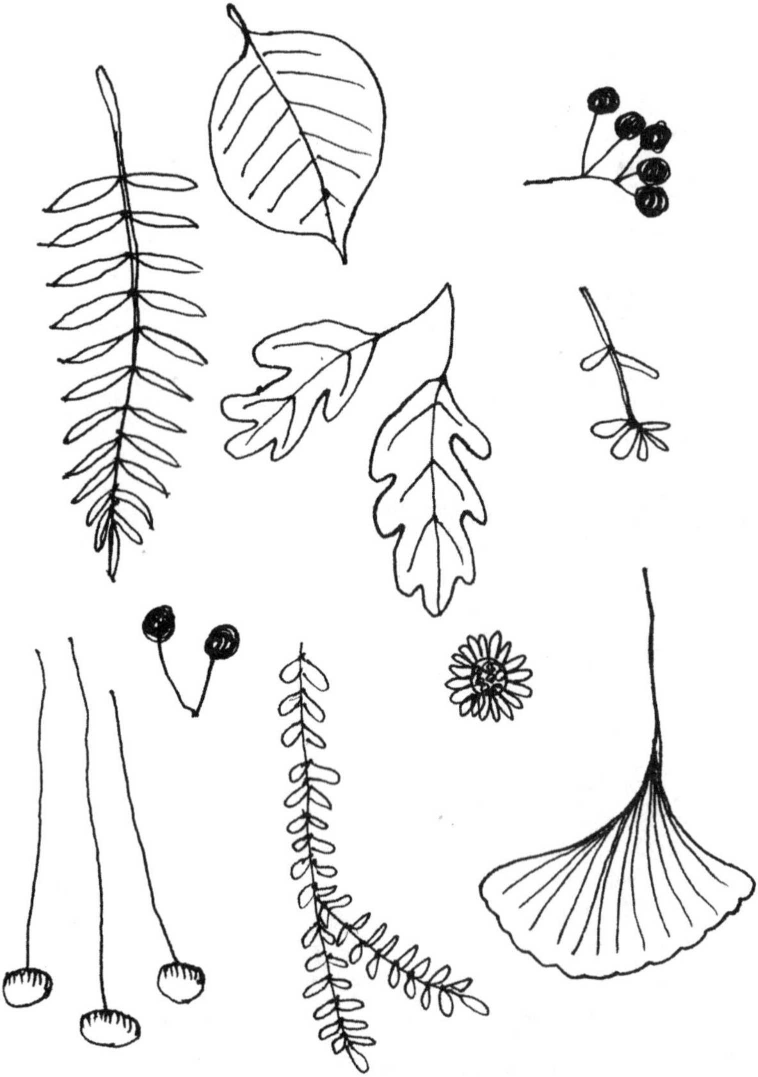

PLANT SCAVENGE

1. Go to a specific outdoor location.

2. Collect as many different kinds of wild plants as you can. (Make sure to avoid poison oak and stinging nettles!) (Note: If it is a place where the flora and fauna are protected, such as a state park, then document with photos.) It may be helpful to use a plant identification guidebook.

3. Arrange your collection and try to identify the plants using a field guide.

Build it up.

Build it up with layers.

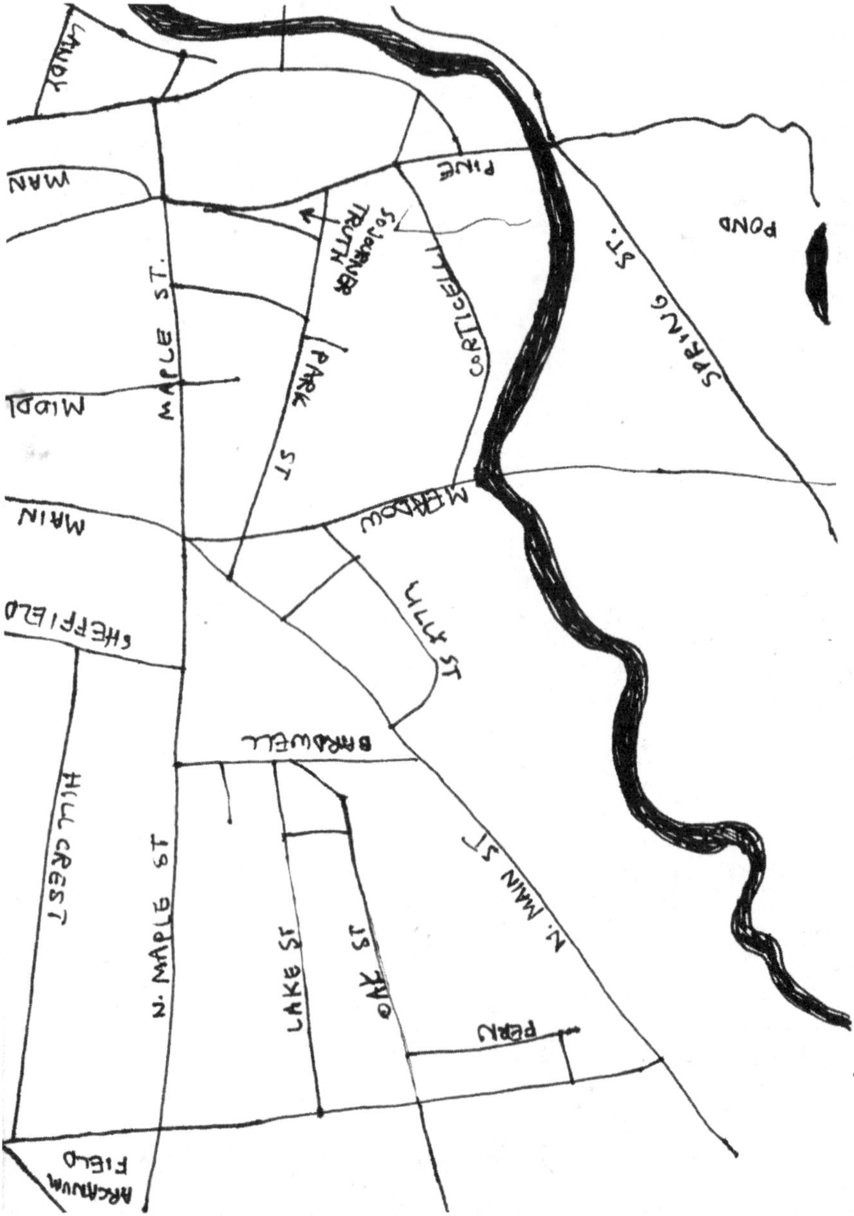
ARCANUM FIELD
FERN
OAK ST
LAKE ST
N. MAPLE ST
HILLCREST
N. MAIN ST
BARDWELL
LILY ST
SHEFFIELD
MAIN
MEADOW
PARK ST
MIDDL
MAPLE ST.
CORTICELLI
SPRING ST.
POND
SOJOURNER TRUTH
PINE
MAN
LANDY

MAP SCAVENGE

1. Choose a specific location with defined boundaries (park, street block).

2. Go for a walk and choose ten objects/landmarks.

3. Create a set of clues for each thing (for example, next to the red fire hydrant, something that is yellow).

4. Give the clues to a friend and have your friend locate each item.

Wild card. Choose an alteration yourself.

Create your own alteration.

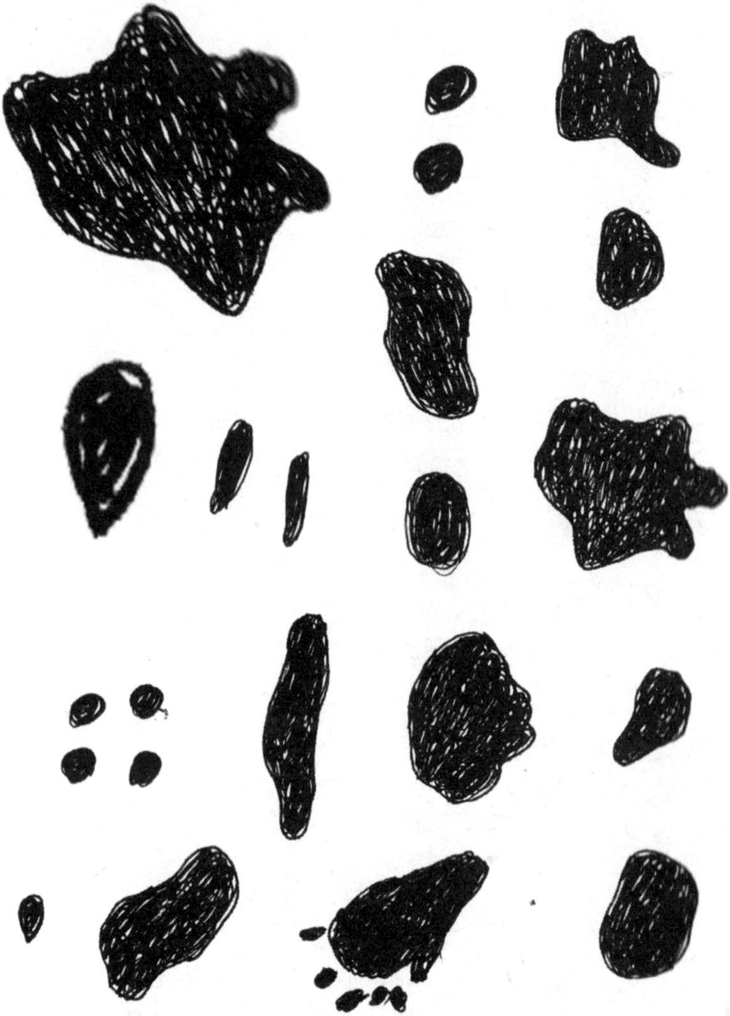

Do something boring.

Fill every square inch with something.

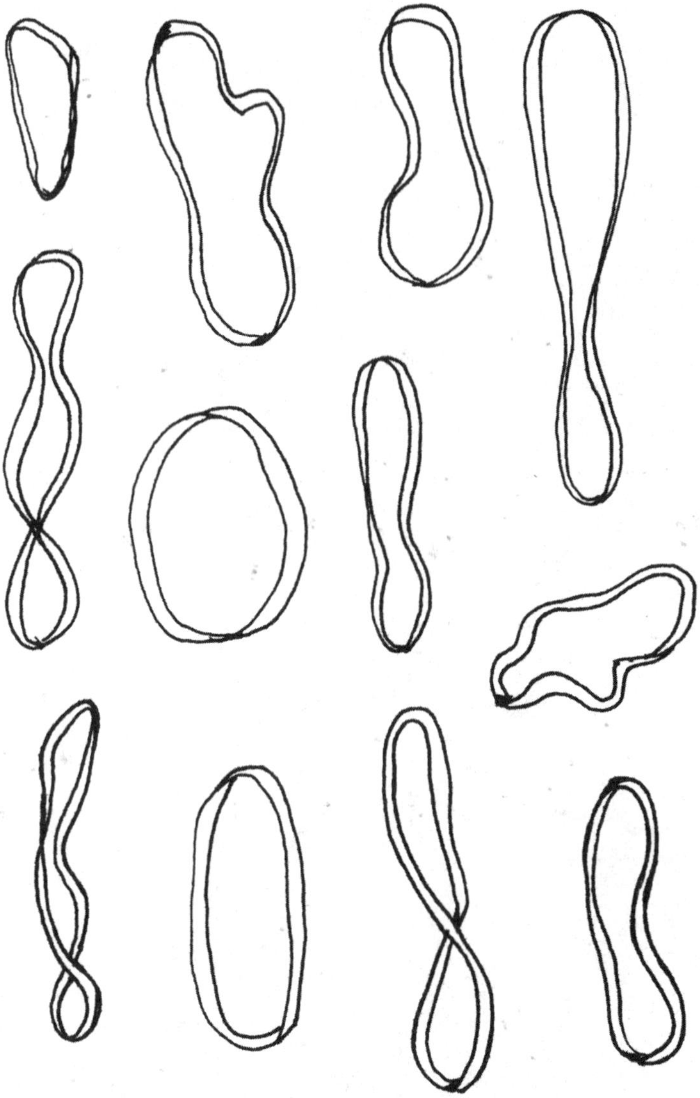

ONE THING SCAVENGE

1. Choose one object to collect or document. (Some ideas: blue things, rubber bands, tickets, stamps, park benches, etc.)

2. Look for the object everywhere you go. Collect or document it in some way.

Go crazy on it.

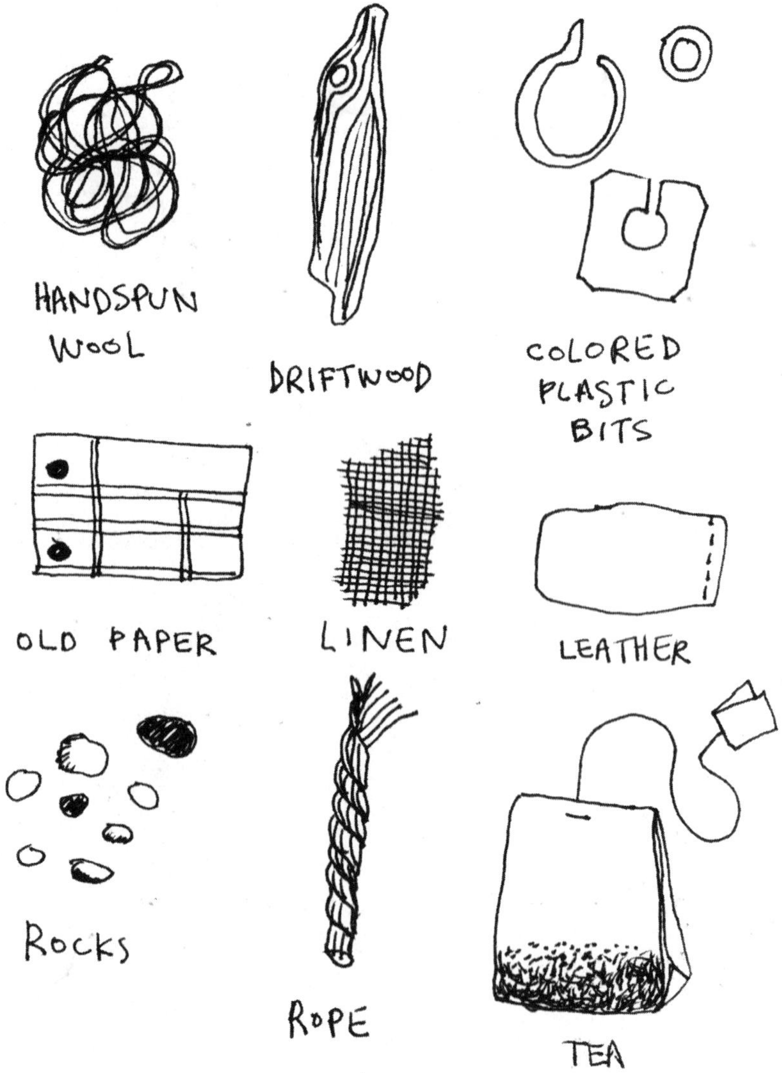
HANDSPUN WOOL
DRIFTWOOD
COLORED PLASTIC BITS
OLD PAPER
LINEN
LEATHER
ROCKS
ROPE
TEA

Draw as slowly as humanly possible.

PERSONAL SCAVENGE

1. Create a scavenge based on your own personal preferences and tastes (for example, find a wrapper from your favorite candy, find a variety of textures you really enjoy).

2. Give it to a friend to use.

Go away for five minutes. Come back and doodle somthing.

Add as many things as you can.

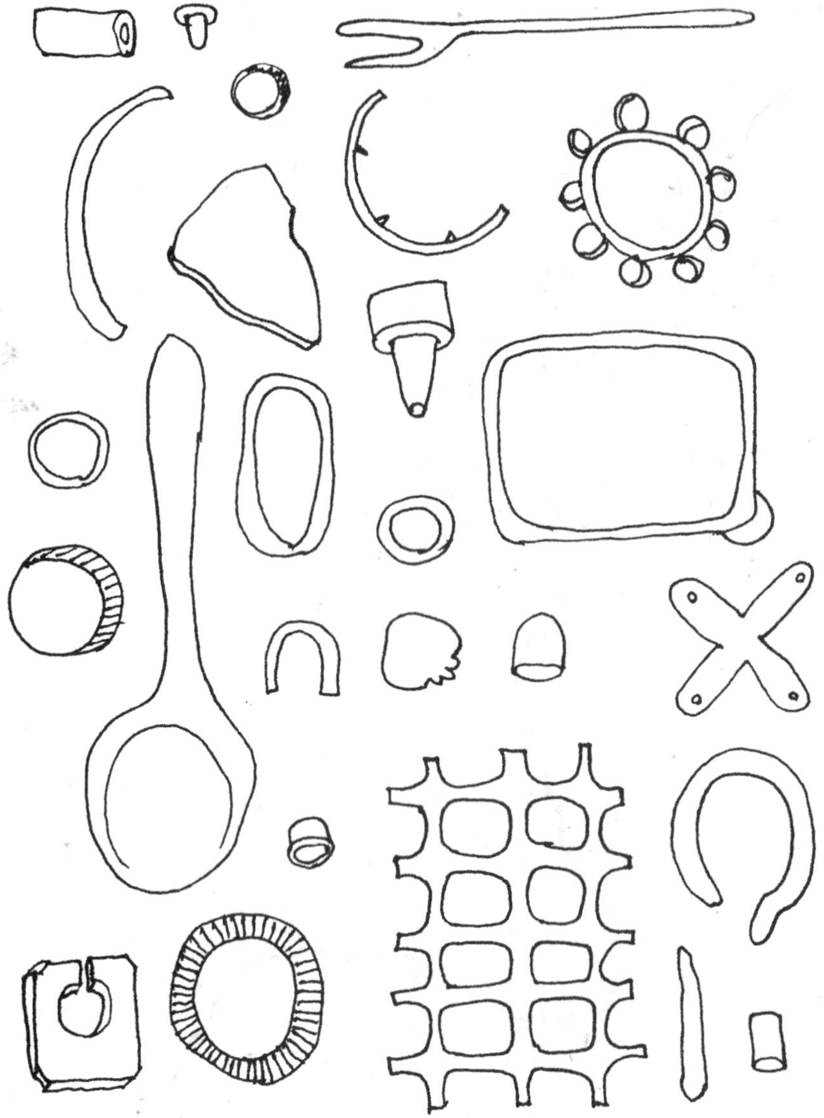

PLASTIC SCAVENGE

1. Collect as many pieces of discarded plastic as you can.

2. Document them separately or as a group.

3. Create some kind of installation with the pieces.

Make part of it pretty and part of it ugly.

MEETING PLACE: THE PARK
SCAVENGE
YOU MUST FIND:
1 CANDY WRAPPER
1 PENNY
4 LEAVES
2 NEWSPAPER CLIPPINGS
1 CRAB APPLE
1 PIECE OF BARK
1 PIECE OF PLASTIC
1 BLADE OF GRASS
1 SAMPLE OF HANDWRITING
2 ACORN HATS

Assemble some art materials. Use them all.

MEETING SCAVENGE

1. Arrange to meet a friend at a specific location.

2. Each person gives a scavenge assignment to the other to collect a predetermined number of objects.

Preserve it.

Incorporate fruit.

LUCY WAS HERE.
1cent
SAM 2001

URBAN FOSSILS

Go out and document as many urban fossils as you can find. These will be things that have been embedded somehow in concrete sidewalks—footprints (animal and human), leaf prints, patterns, coins, names, etc.

Photograph it. Include photo.

CHECKLIST

QUICK REFERENCE LIST OF ITEMS

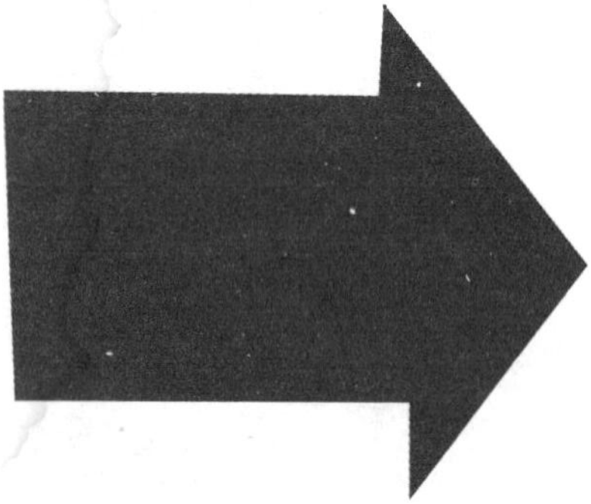

Make a statement.

Turn it into something that flies.

- ☐ POSTAGE STAMPS
- ☐ THE NUMBER FIVE
- ☐ A PAPER CLIP
- ☐ A FEATHER
- ☐ A USED ENVELOPE
- ☐ A TICKET
- ☐ NINE CIRCLES
- ☐ CURRENCY
- ☐ SEE THROUGH
- ☐ THREE DIFFERENT TEXTURES
- ☐ TEXT
- ☐ A POST-IT NOTE
- ☐ A PIECE OF MOSS
- ☐ SOME WIRE
- ☐ SOMETHING YOU ATE
- ☐ LOCAL ENVIRONMENT
- ☐ ON YOUR BODY
- ☐ A USED TEA BAG
- ☐ A NAPKIN
- ☐ SOMETHING STICKY
- ☐ SIX BLUE THINGS
- ☐ PUZZLE PIECE
- ☐ AN ELASTIC BAND
- ☐ CHARACTER
- ☐ SEVERAL LEAVES
- ☐ RED STRING
- ☐ A WRAPPER
- ☐ A PHOTO OF YOURSELF
- ☐ A POSTCARD
- ☐ FOUR SQUARES
- ☐ FIVE BUTTONS
- ☐ ELEPHANT
- ☐ ROCK TRACINGS
- ☐ SOMETHING ORANGE
- ☐ YEAR YOU WERE BORN
- ☐ HANDWRITTEN QUOTE
- ☐ FIVE SAMPLES HANDWRITING
- ☐ GRAVESTONE RUBBING
- ☐ A HAIR SAMPLE
- ☐ FORTUNE
- ☐ COUPON
- ☐ SOMETHING BROKEN
- ☐ SOMETHING DISCARDED
- ☐ LIQUID STAIN
- ☐ GREEN STAIN
- ☐ SOMETHING CRUMBLED
- ☐ SOMETHING DRAGGED
- ☐ PART OF A TREE
- ☐ SOMETHING PLANTED
- ☐ A FOUND NOTE
- ☐ FLAT CANDY
- ☐ SEED PODS
- ☐ LEFT BY AN ANIMAL
- ☐ MACHINE MADE
- ☐ HANDMADE
- ☐ MINIATURE
- ☐ ORIGAMI
- ☐ GIVEN TO YOU
- ☐ DRAWING
- ☐ GRASS
- ☐ IMAGINARY
- ☐ STYROFOAM
- ☐ PLASTIC
- ☐ SPOTS
- ☐ SOMETHING CURVED
- ☐ SIX TRIANGLES
- ☐ HOLE IN IT
- ☐ PART OF A BOOK
- ☐ BOTTOM OF SHOE
- ☐ CONSTRUCTION SITE
- ☐ UPC SYMBOL
- ☐ GREEN FABRIC

What would it say if it could talk?

THIS PAGE IS RESERVED FOR A

MYSTERY OBJECT*

* AN OBJECT YOU FIND WHILE ON A SCAVENGE THAT IS NOT ON THE LIST BUT IS TOO GOOD TO PASS UP.

LOCATION FOUND: ____________

TIME: ______ DATE: ________

STORY: ____________________

Add a paper bag.

BIBLIOGRAPHY

Abram, David. *The Spell of the Sensuous*. New York: Vintage, 1997.

Bachelard, Gaston. *The Poetics of Space*. Boston: Beacon Press, 1994.

Buchanan-Smith, Peter. *Speck: A Curious Collection of Uncommon Things*. New York: Princeton Architectural Press, 2001.

Elpel, Thomas J. *Botany in a Day: The Patterns Method of Plant Identification*. Pony, Montana: HOPS Press, 2004.

Fletcher, Allan. *The Art of Looking Sideways*. New York: Phaidon Press, 2001.

Fletcher, Allan. *Picturing and Poeting*. New York: Phaidon Press, 2006.

Gooley, Tristan. *The Natural Navigator*. New York: The Experiment, 2010.

Harmon, Katherine. *You Are Here: Personal Geographies and Other Maps of the Imagination*. New York: Princeton Architectural Press, 2003.

Jernigan, Candy. *Evidence: The Art of Candy Jernigan*. San Francisco: Chronicle Books, 1999.

Create a collage.

Johnstone, Stephen (editor). The Everyday. Boston: MIT Press, 2008.

Kent, Corita. Learning by Heart. Allworth Press: 2008.

Munari, Bruno. From Afar It Was an Island. Verona, Italy: Corraini, 1971.

Munari, Bruno. The Sea as Craftsman. Mantova Italy, 1995.

Munari, Bruno. The Tactile Workshops. Mantova Italy, 1985.

Perec, Georges. The Species of Spaces and Other Pieces. New York: Penguin, 2008.

Tuan, Yi-Fu. Space and Place: The Perspective of Experience. Boston: Beacon Press, 1994.

Wilde, Ann and Jürgen Wilde (editors). Karl Blossfeldt: Working Collages. Boston: MIT Press, 2001.

Documentary Films

The Gleaners and I by Agnès Varda

Waste Land by Lucy Walker, João Jardim, and Karen Harley

Invite a bunch of friends.

AVAILABLE FROM PENGUIN BOOKS

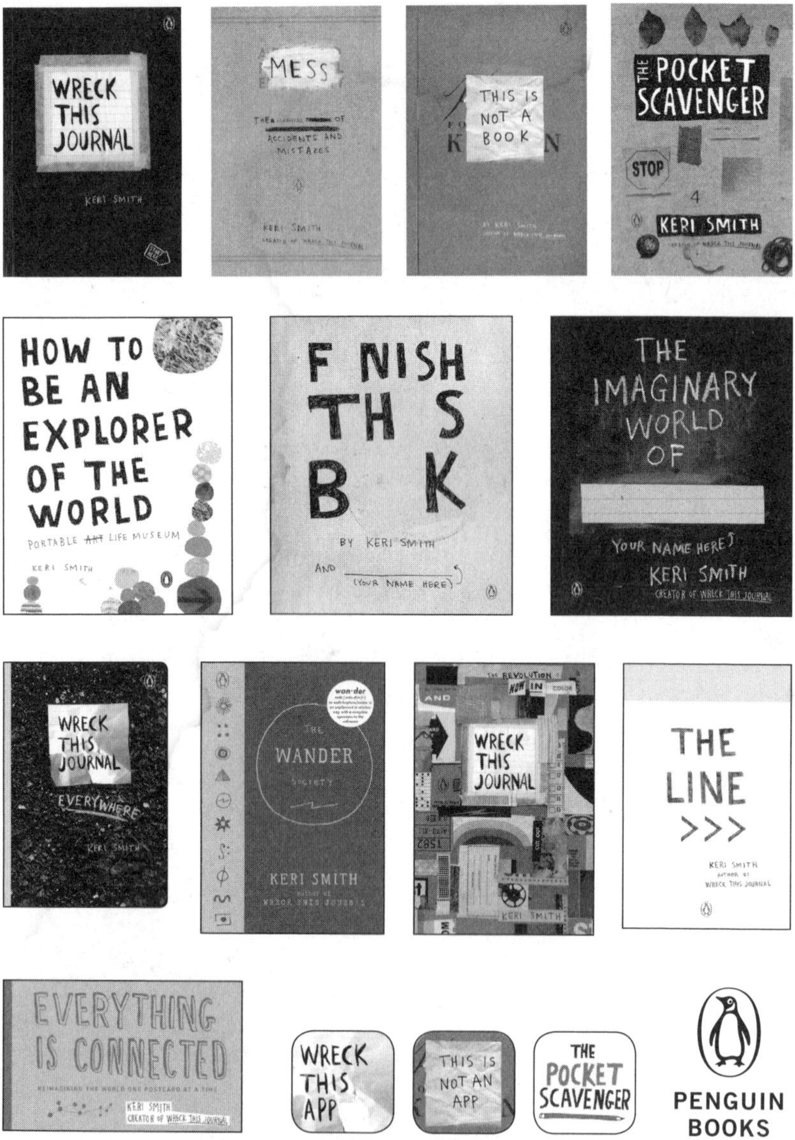
WRECK THIS JOURNAL
KERI SMITH
MESS
ACCIDENTS AND MISTAKES
KERI SMITH
THIS IS NOT A BOOK
THE POCKET SCAVENGER
STOP
KERI SMITH
HOW TO BE AN EXPLORER OF THE WORLD
PORTABLE ART LIFE MUSEUM
KERI SMITH
FINISH THIS BOOK
BY KERI SMITH
AND (YOUR NAME HERE)
THE IMAGINARY WORLD OF
YOUR NAME HERE
KERI SMITH
CREATOR OF WRECK THIS JOURNAL
WRECK THIS JOURNAL
EVERYWHERE
KERI SMITH
THE WANDER SOCIETY
KERI SMITH
THE REVOLUTION IS NOW IN COLOR
WRECK THIS JOURNAL
KERI SMITH
THE LINE
>>>
KERI SMITH
AUTHOR OF WRECK THIS JOURNAL
EVERYTHING IS CONNECTED
REIMAGINING THE WORLD ONE POSTCARD AT A TIME
KERI SMITH
CREATOR OF WRECK THIS JOURNAL
WRECK THIS APP
THIS IS NOT AN APP
THE POCKET SCAVENGER
PENGUIN BOOKS

Add the sun.